Fascinating INSECTS

Spiders

Aaron Carr

LET'S READ AV² BY WEIGL ADDED VALUE • AUDIO VISUAL

www.av2books.com

Go to www.av2books.com, and enter this book's unique code.

BOOK CODE

B407416

AV² by Weigl brings you media enhanced books that support active learning.

AV² provides enriched content that supplements and complements this book. Weigl's AV² books strive to create inspired learning and engage young minds in a total learning experience.

Your AV² Media Enhanced books come alive with...

Audio
Listen to sections of the book read aloud.

Video
Watch informative video clips.

Embedded Weblinks
Gain additional information for research.

Try This!
Complete activities and hands-on experiments.

Key Words
Study vocabulary, and complete a matching word activity.

Quizzes
Test your knowledge.

Slide Show
View images and captions, and prepare a presentation.

... and much, much more!

Published by AV² by Weigl
350 5th Avenue, 59th Floor New York, NY 10118
Website: www.av2books.com www.weigl.com

Library of Congress Control Number: 2013937275
ISBN 978-1-62127-330-1 (hardcover)
ISBN 978-1-62127-335-6 (softcover)

Printed in the United States of America in North Mankato, Minnesota
1 2 3 4 5 6 7 8 9 0 17 16 15 14 13

052013
WEP040413

Project Coordinator: Aaron Carr Art Director: Terry Paulhus

Weigl acknowledges Getty Images as the primary image supplier for this title.

Spiders

CONTENTS

Meet the spider.

Spiders are small animals.
They have eight legs.

Spiders can be found
all around the world.

All around the world,
most spiders live alone.

Spiders are born
when they hatch from eggs.

When they are born, some spiders ride on their mother's back.

Spiders spin webs made of silk.

With webs made of silk,
some spiders make their own homes.

Spiders have two long fangs.

With two long fangs, spiders can keep themselves safe.

Spiders may have
four pairs of eyes.

With four pairs of eyes,
spiders can see all around them.

Spiders eat insects.

By eating insects, spiders get
all the food they need to be healthy.

Spiders hunt to catch their food.

To catch their food,
some spiders spin webs as traps.

Spiders are important in nature.

In nature, spiders help
keep pest numbers down.

SPIDER FACTS

These pages provide more detail about the interesting facts found in the book. They are intended to be used by adults as a learning support to help young readers round out their knowledge of each insect or arachnid featured in the *Fascinating Insects* series.

Pages 4–5

Spiders are small animals. They belong to a group of animals called arachnids. Arachnids are related to insects but have some key differences. Arachnids have eight jointed legs and bodies with two parts: the abdomen and cephalothorax. The cephalothorax is a combined head and upper body. There are more than 43,000 species of spiders. They range in size from 0.02 to 3.5 inches (0.5 to 90 millimeters) long. Female spiders can be up to twice as large as males.

Pages 6–7

Spiders live in almost all parts of the world. They can be found on all continents except Antarctica. Most spider species live in tropical zones, though many inhabit temperate regions as well. Spiders can be found in the Himalayas at elevations up to 16,400 feet (5,000 meters), and other species have adapted to life in water. The diving bell spider spins a web around itself and traps air inside. This allows the spider to breathe while underwater.

Pages 8–9

Spiders hatch from eggs when they are born. Spiders put their eggs in an egg sac, which can hold up to 1,000 eggs. When the eggs hatch, the baby spiders, called spiderlings, look like full-grown spiders but smaller. Some spiderlings take care of themselves right away. Others ride on their mother's back. As the spiderlings grow, they molt, or shed their skin. Spiders are fully grown after about one year.

Pages 10–11

Spiders spin webs made of silk. Depending on the species, spiders may have six or more silk glands. These glands make silk, which spiders then spin into webs. They use special organs called spinnerets to spin their webs. Many types of spiders use their webs to make homes for themselves. They also use the webs to help them catch food.

Pages 12–13

Spiders have two long fangs. Spiders will use their fangs for self defence when they have to, but most spiders use their fangs for hunting and eating. The fangs are located on each side of the spider's jaw. In most spiders, the jaw opens sideways in a pinching motion. In tarantula-like spiders, the jaw moves forward and down. Spiders use their fangs to capture, and even eat, their prey. The fangs are hollow to allow the spider to inject venom into its prey. The venom either paralyzes or kills the prey.

Pages 14–15

Spiders have four pairs of eyes. Most spiders have eight eyes arranged in pairs. Some species have fewer eyes, and a few underground species do not have eyes. There are usually two large eyes on the front of the cephalothorax and smaller eyes on the sides. However, different species have eyes arranged in different sizes and positions. The large, or main, eyes do most of the work. The smaller, or secondary, eyes can only detect the direction light comes from.

Pages 16–17

Spiders eat insects. Almost all spiders are carnivores. They mostly eat insects, though some of the larger species of tarantulas are known to eat rodents, frogs, lizards, and bats. Spiders turn their food to liquid before eating it. Most spiders use their fangs to inject digestive juices into their prey. This turns the prey to liquid. The spider then uses its fangs like straws to suck up its food.

Pages 18–19

Spiders hunt to catch their food. Some spider species are active hunters. They go searching for their food. These spiders follow prey until they get within 2 to 4 inches (5 to 10 centimeters). Then, they jump to capture their prey. Other spiders hide in leaves or flowers of the same color as the spiders. However, most spiders are passive hunters. This means they simply wait for their prey to stumble onto their webs and become stuck.

Pages 20–21

Spiders are important in nature. As one of the largest groups of predators that prey on insects, spiders play a very important role in maintaining healthy and balanced ecosystems. Spiders are even used on farms and in gardens to help control pest populations. Some farmers believe that spiders provide a safe and natural way to protect their crops.

KEY WORDS

Research has shown that as much as 65 percent of all written material published in English is made up of 300 words. These 300 words cannot be taught using pictures or learned by sounding them out. They must be recognized by sight. This book contains 47 common sight words to help young readers improve their reading fluency and comprehension. This book also teaches young readers several important content words. These words are paired with pictures to aid in learning and improve understanding.

Page	Sight Words First Appearance
4	the
5	animals, are, have, small, they
7	all, around, be, can, found, live, most, world
8	from, when
9	back, mother's, on, some, their
10	made, of
11	homes, make, own, with
12	long, two
13	keep
14	eyes, four, may
15	see, them
16	by, eat, food, get, need, to
19	as
20	down, help, important, in, numbers

Page	Content Words First Appearance
4	spider
5	legs
8	eggs
10	silk, webs
12	fangs
14	pairs
16	insects
19	traps
20	nature, pest